THE
WIFE'S
ACCOUNT

POETRY BY ESTA SPALDING

Carrying Place
Anchoress
Lost August

THE
WIFE'S
ACCOUNT

poems

ESTA
SPALDING

Anansi

Published in Canada in 2002 by
House of Anansi Press Limited
895 Don Mills Rd., 400-2 Park Centre
Toronto, ON, M3C 1W3
Tel. (416) 445-3333
Fax (416) 445-5967
www.anansi.ca

Distributed in Canada by
General Distribution Services Ltd.
325 Humber College Blvd.
Etobicoke, ON, M9W 7C3
Tel. (416) 213-1919
Fax (416) 213-1917
E-mail cservice@genpub.com

06 05 04 03 02   1 2 3 4 5

NATIONAL LIBRARY OF CANADA CATALOGUING IN PUBLICATION DATA

Spalding, Esta
The wife's account

Poems.
ISBN 0-88784-675-0

I. Title.

PS8587.P214W44 2002   C811'.54   C2002-900333-4
PR9199.3.S63W44 2002

Cover Image: Halton Archive/Getty Images   Typesetting: Brian Panhuyzen
Printed and bound in Canada

THE CANADA COUNCIL | LE CONSEIL DES ARTS
FOR THE ARTS | DU CANADA
SINCE 1957 | DEPUIS 1957

*We acknowledge for their financial support of our publishing program the Canada
Council for the Arts, the Ontario Arts Council, and the Government of Canada
through the Book Publishing Industry Development Program (BPIDP).*

Contents

Voice, come out of the silence
Say something.
Appear in the form of a spider
Or a moth beating the curtain.

Dark hollows said, lee to the wind,
The moon said, back of an eel,
The salt said, look by the sea,
Your tears are not enough praise,
You will find no comfort here,
In the kingdom of bang and blab.

— from "The Lost Son"

One

i. Matins

Look at them in bed in the blue of early morning.
Look how he presses against her, his knees bending
where her knees bend, his stomach & chest against her back.
His breath, warm & light, against her neck. The bottom sheet
pulling off the mattress, but holding. Dog snorts &
lifts his head, alarm bleats & the husband
presses the button for the fourth time this morning. She's
been awake since it first went off.
The dog on her numb arm, she wants to shift but
the dog will jump up, his bladder's full,
husband jump up, he's late for work, instead
she holds still, thinks her way back into sleep: she was trying
to buy her mother a wig, but the train didn't come. In the dream
she kissed her mother's head, bald as an infant's. Something
about placing her hands on either side of her mother's
skull. Something about the warm skin against her lips
like the light — just now — through the blinds

ii. Notorious

What they say of me is true:
I was pulled from mountain ice

my mouth stopped blue
where the river entered

It was January
days of sanctity & refusal

(For a long time I'd dreamt my heart into a fish
poised in a jar on a shelf in my chest)

Iced over & stopped
torpor entered

The way a lover enters cellular
& secrets himself in every chamber

I had been dead one hundred & twenty-two
minutes long enough to get to the part

where 'Alicia' escapes down the staircase
The physician snapped his other glove adjusted

the gauze over his mouth with exacting
steel he cleaved my chest

& lifted the jar
unscrewing the lid

Beneath the ice
the fish & the luck to find

He's not on the stairs
take them two at a time

out of the ruined castle into blue night
The ice escaped my body

as I escaped my body — in bliss
golden-finned

iii.

Nothing he said would leave her

his hands on her hips

left small scars his words

a long scarf that will catch

he said whatever came

into his head

something about information

theory: snow on the limbs

of a winter tree almost a grammar

of that body She thought he

meant her arms & legs

She was self-conscious

He kissed her trunk

left once again

a sentence mostly unfinished

little pieces of himself

on the branches

iv.

Sun's come again & with it
wind that lifts the pretty girls'

skirts — every one a Marilyn
doe-eyed & drugged.

Your mother drowned
in the bathtub her hair plugging

the drain. All the women you loved
left you this way.

The time we drove to America —
to Buffalo *home of the first electric chair*

wind carried a storm
of locusts — the wipers smeared

green bodies across the glass & you
couldn't look past. I was

enough America for you —
you never held me

as hard as
I wanted you to.

Sun's come & with it
rain. The lying daffodils.

Have I said, wish you
would take my hair

into your mouth?
Enough for a nest.

v. Letters from My Other Self

She writes from the middle of winter
> *wool of the dead lamb gives*
> *the neck of every sweater I've knit*
> *since Epiphany*

she's got a pain not even
> *the dying wolves in the dying*
> *hills could hunger away*

the cow dead a month, rotting
in the forgotten Deepfreeze
she'd pulled the plug by mistake
the city dump, loud with vultures
though she's deaf to anything but
the cow's hum & vibration
> *a skull picked clean's*
> *an instrument in wind*

her reedy fingers on the pen — words
fleshless, all industry & cunning
letters knit as an animal is slaughtered
& spun
> *the amaryllis dragged*
> *too early from sleep*
> *curls round its red*
> *tongues swallowing itself*

she draws back her shoulders
opening an ivory fan
> *twilight's the best time*

when the trees take up their shadows
like girls at a dance
lifting their skirts
moving thin into darkness

vi. *"That painting of the saints"*

Is it true the house is
burning & all the saints still
seated at the table
bread on their plates, glasses
half-empty
half-full of wine? Is it
the woman under the table who
washes each foot, who washes
later the dishes?
You are in the kitchen
making risotto when I look
up from the book where the house
is burning &
you want to know
if you should barbecue fennel.
The refugees
leave their burning rooms
& on CNN eighteen thousand
citizens gather to save
the last bridge in Belgrade
from the bombs.
A woman washes their feet
in river water?
One saint lifts his glass
to the erased space where his head
once was —

his gold-leaf robe
falls from absent shoulders —
that detail destroyed
in a flood that turned
the river flesh-coloured.
In his hand the glass
that toasts a table spread
with bread & knives.

vii. Jericho Easter

Fifty straight days of rain.
Then the sky shuts tight
a boulder rolled
across the mouth of a cave.

At Jericho Beach the woman waves
her metal detector, cocking her
ear to the secret currents
(the way that saint
in old paintings
leans toward a window, pregnant
with light).

She marches
behind a tide that slips
over every horizon.

Sweeping the air above the sand
her noise, the hum of summer
when the sun rises, bringing
water to a boil.
It's that decidedly yellow.

This is March: wedding ring, car
keys, teaspoon, crucifix, skeleton
of an umbrella.

viii.

There's only one plot
D's ex tells me
outside Starbucks on a wrought
iron bench (me anxious
having given up coffee)
What's that? I ask real polite
A stranger arrives she says just as
one does
bumping into her &
knocking a double tall
latte onto her coat
Next time use a lid
she cautions the stranger
stooping to the empty cup
a small scar on the back of her neck
Where was I? the ex asks
wringing out her scarf
a gift from D
long before he met me

ix.

In the morning two roses in
a thin ceramic vase by the bed
twin sisters from that childhood story
Rose Red & Rose White
who were pricked & bled
& fell asleep in glass coffins

later waking to twin husbands

A new frog in D's tank has laid eggs
long strings of jelly with little black eyes
none of the captive frogs will fertilize
such is life behind glass

Walking the beach at the tip of the peninsula
I notice the nudists have erected
a dazzling tinfoil amphitheatre
that will fortify their tans

like shadows on a sundial
each hour they move a few degrees
clockwise —

Telling this at Easter dinner
I am chastised by a nudist friend
They don't want you gawking

The rules so complicated
second degree burns on my wrist
lifting the scalding pan of tofu-chicken
from the oven

Conversation turns to the man with full use
of his legs who entered the wheelchair race
took third place & then was disqualified

Everyone outraged at God or the judges
maybe not in the sky anymore

tonight twin roses unfurl
above our sleeping heads

x. *You Are in the Embrace of History*

His most beautiful wife
Nefertari
all the servants told her
so calling her *beautiful*
with tall twin plumes
saying *One is pleased with*
what comes forth
concerning her
History asks, did
she give him sons?
If so, which ones? Loved
even more in death
buried in her own tomb
in the *Place of Beauty* also called
Valley of Queens (there were
many) frescoes on the walls
of her tomb that after
flooding calcified
the plaster lifting
off though custom dictated
that the actual lives
of royal wives
went unrecorded &
what exists is in
the nether world

Married at fifteen
his first wife *mistress*
of Upper & Lower Egypt
beloved of the vulture Mut
beloved wife dipped
in honey after death
one lives — the artisan carved
into her tomb —
just to hear her voice

xi.   Bringing the Queen's Tomb to Light

Did she live or was she just a
story, a figure carved in a perspective
our eyes cannot make out? Gently,

gently brush back the dirt & take
her measure. Each feature — face, waist, legs —
rendered at its most descriptive angle,
so her body appears twisted — nose in profile, yet
her shoulders straight.
How else to know the beloved?

          That afternoon in the
airport when we first said goodbye (later
there would be other goodbyes, but I did not know
this as you walked down the long man-built tunnel
into the belly of the machine) & you
turned, blinking in the blinking light, you
squinted back, your face in profile — one
eye, that face I knew to hover above me, a planet — you
waved your one free hand.

I did not know airplane, understood only
that you were going into sky —

Who was I without you?
Born to say goodbye
& your plane — I thought of it as your plane — lifted off, nose up,
carving a heaven-blue wall
                    Goodbye, mother,
Queen of the sky, bride
of the bird, goodbye.

xii.

This morning I counted fourteen pigeons
on the telephone wire, heads cocked

in the same direction as if listening
to the same conversation, as if overhearing

the call telling me you were gone.
Fourteen pigeons. Half the number of years

you walked on this earth. Must be something
to that, I thought, looking where their faces pointed

to the rooftops on the other side of the park.
You were somewhere

beyond those houses, somewhere
surrounded by a sky that always fills

its edges. How many other times
did you reach me through that wire?

xiii. Occupant

All afternoon the sun paints the room.

Beginning on the far wall its brushes
moving slowly, slowly
toward then along the floor dragging
the shadows with it.

Shadow of table
shadow of sixteen chair legs
shadow of humped sofa
rectangular shadow of the leather trunk
even the crucifix shadow of windowpanes.
                              I lie
watching these dark, distorted
versions of their weighted selves

ghost the room.

At three o'clock for just a moment the sun
pauses on my flat, breathing form.

Where was I? While someone else
was putting on my shoes, buttoning the last
button of my winter coat, where was I?

xiv. Interior

In dark woods, I confuse
the lesson taught me — circa age ten —
on being raped
with instructions on bear attack.
Mother's voice,
like scout instructor's, comes back
Pick your nose, pick
your nose & act retarded. That'll
stop him in his tracks.

The small cabin set beside the fresh-minted
lake. Lace up boots, slide on pack (bottled water
sunscreen   insect repellent) head into
bear country.
Pine trees, like enlarged air fresheners.
Nice man with fishing rod
says *Shake a can of rocks.* Husband
unhelpful, identifying wildflowers   *bastard*
toadflax   bastard toadflax
High above another eagle sizing us up.

People drive here from Florida to see
bears & we go to Florida to see
alligators.
                    People in minivans crisscrossing

the continent, making lists of exotic licence plates.
Picking their noses at stoplights or on straightaways —

Come to think of it, we're asking for it
& those teeth.

xv. On Gnawing

Tea on the deck with slices of bread & cheese, hummus too. D fights the bees for the last berries in the bowl. The dog gnawing on the leg of an animal who dragged furrows across these fields until a few days ago.

Talking Crown politics & politics of ducks, sheep & peacocks, not to mention the chickens with twisted feet. D, reluctant vegetarian, says that at the worst farms they have such deformed legs they lie down for the few short months before slaughter.

This spring's peacocks have all died, eight of them gone to ground. The summer, too wet. From the field appears Jesus, the five-month-old black ram. White face & four white ankles.

My animal will not let me take the bone from his mouth, guards it with sharpened teeth. To write. To write not for anything but the pleasure of gnawing. The pressure of the wrist & fingers, catching ache, a summer with too much water, that colour of blue I can never get down.

A heron lands in the pasture stepping off the air — a businessman adjusting his wings, lapels of a blazer. He steps between ducks toward the business of the pond.

Later, by lamplight, I find a gnawed bone tucked under our pillow, confront D about secret meat-eating. The guilty party sleeping at the foot of the bed.

xvi.

Because mind loves
        body
lumbering as an enormous
        upright bass

He pays an extra fare
        for it on
the bus, arriving at the
        concert hall

snapping back the metal
        hinges
& opening the hard plastic
        case (like

a coffin) he puts rosin
        to the bow
untwists the butterfly
        bolt, extending

a metal finger from
        the bass's base
then with that horse-
        hair bow, mind

tells body a story (it is
          a story body
can live with) once,
          it says,

a girl's body ran across
          Poland
She had a picture
          in her mind

of a barn her mother had
          painted
in a dream
          the girl ran

for days & nights
          days & nights until
she found the barn
          & — surprise —

the girl's brother
          was inside
Because mind needs
          body

he sends it
        flowers
he pretends to be a
        long lost brother

mind loves body
        to insist
they are not the same
        thing

xvii. Hinge

You lie beside me
sand on the back of your arms
& legs   your back
grains in your hair & behind your ears

Around us the susurration of ocean
an airplane overhead
open scissors through unstaunched sky

by my right ear & looking so much
like an ear the curve of a clamshell broken
its pieces scattered
but still that unmistakable whorl
once home to muscle that closed
the shell (all of it: muscle   shell
soft tissue of hinge
the same animal it protected)

Now the indelicate crows
lifting closed shells & dropping
them onto asphalt

The young seagull
beats his wings over the abandoned
plate of chicken
his beak shreds the tendon of another
fuelling flight

He will be carried away
by his own cravings
as I made my life with this man
the one who walked up to me at a party
he was someone else's
but the shape his hands made in air when he spoke
was a place to put my grief

That man whose head touches my head in the sand
whose eyes open to the same clawed sky

xviii.   Fate

Twice that night I found the cat
in the garage circling the one-eyed mouse.

The first time I chased the cat
under the car. Then scooping
the mouse into my cupped palms
I walked out under a blind
moon & dropped Mister One-Eye
in a plot of clover.

When I went into the garage later
they were there again — scripted
enemies in some second-rate sequel.

That time I picked up the cat.
Scolding him. Asking that he be
a little more civil.
If you come into the house,
I'll open you a can
of cow's liver.

xix.

For days the man & woman
have been silent.

Only the hum of the fridge or
click of the electric kettle

switching off once it's come
to a boil.

In the past, they've dragged
talk into the air, chains

of words, like the curved
monkeys

the child will someday
lift arm in arm from a barrel.

Now stillness.
Because it is done.

A thing accomplished.
Their own bodies, even

their tongues, exhausted.
Now the air full of mingled breath.

Now sunlight paints the kitchen.
Now crow, stationed in the pine, rustles once

& waits —

Two

i.

It was the one thing
         I would not speak about.
It was that jungle cat who
         hunches over the river, taking
a thick clawed paw & tapping the taut
         surface of the water, drawing
up the fish. The same cat will lean
         all four tense, muscled legs forward
stretch its neck over the water & dip
         the tips of its whiskers in
like antenna, listening, listening
         for hints of movement in the hurrying stream.

It was the one thing I would not speak about.
         So when it called, I had no choice.

I rose to the surface, unaware
         of the listening whiskers, unaware
of the poised claws.

         Listen. I must tell you this —

ii.

This time when we make love we
take the wooded path, venturing further
into the tea-stained dark
& so we happen together
on the riverbank.
After love comes more love, a longer
deeper river. Into the cold-rushing, trout-
speckled water, we toss
a stone, asking that it carve
our names into the great granite river wall.
Now splashing a little onto
ourselves (entering a temple) we turn
from the river toward home.
In this manner, we come to an unfamiliar
room: a long-carpeted hall whose
walls have been eased down,
whose formal paintings (here a bowl
of apples, there a bending dancer)
hang from stars. Look up,
there is no ceiling, look down
(near the wooden desk where
the poem sits half-finished)
— a firefly aches with light.

iii.

Worried what to eat, I stopped
coffee. An animal craving animal, I
considered meat.

No herbal tea
with its pollens.
No wine.
I did everything right (put a filter
on the tap against chlorine).

Expectation, the narrative.
A clock without a face.

So this is stillness, the life
of body.

The queen who chews off her
wings, I
wanted nothing.

You don't believe me?
Ask the gods if I was quiet.

iv. The Key

While the men in the office continue their never-ending
        deconstruction of Scorcese, she
takes the key from where it hangs, on the hook &
        goes down the hall to the women's washroom —
the one next door to the Birthright clinic where girls who
        have read the ads in buses *Pregnant? Need*
Help? leave with a stuffed bunny for the baby — & she unbuttons
        wool pants, letting her stomach expand completely for
the first time all morning. Then pushing her cotton panties
        down, she sits on the toilet — institutional, like the
toilets in hospitals — & bleeds.
        They have told her this only means the child
is threatened. Like weather, the pain is
        coming now, building at the base of her back, rolling
up her spine & off her shoulders, so she leans
        her head between her knees, her hair dragging on the floor,
now she can hear another woman outside, fiddling with
        the key, jiggling the lock & so she calls out *Just a minute* the
blood, she sees, tilting her face to the bowl, is crumbling out,
        bricks from a ruined fortress. Overhead, the fan's
dull rumble scatters dust like ashes & the tick
        as one blade catches each time it sweeps
past. One more wave & she crumples the paper in her hand
        wiping the sweat from her face, then wiping the blood. She
stands, ready to go back to where the men are discussing
        the scene with the baseball bat & the body
in the trunk of the Cadillac.

v. The Orchard

That afternoon in the orchard
we threw our hats into the air
promising ourselves if they came
back to earth we would last

      Night was a horse we rode

a black horse, carrying a message:

the heart, an apple, whole
before the worm-eaten path
before the intricate hollownesses

Remember the two of us
hats in the air
& under our feet the green
globes of apples

We were childless
& we were happy

What could possibly be
different now?

vi.

You desired &
so you lost.
Need no hospital bed
to tell you this.
No bucket, heavy
in the hands of
the attendant.

Teach me, my bed,
to be as you are.
Your iron bars
cold & thin with
refusals.

Teach me, before I step
into air yellow with
the incinerator's
smoke.

*

Like breath,
for a moment
that molecule
entered.

It might have been
from the body of Caesar
it might have been
Lady Di whose
cells still lace the collars & cuffs
of dresses that hang in museums.

*

I woke in the hospital saying
(to myself) This is not
your life.
                    This is just like
the time you brought
the wrong suitcase
home from the airport
& unzipping it on your bed
discovered dozens & dozens
of pink button-down shirts.

vii.

There it is. In the bowl. She can see it beneath her, could if she wanted, fish it out with her own hands. & it is fishy, is like some small, delicate prawn, though bloodier, as if it's had its shell removed. She says its name, one she's been preparing, name she's been rolling over & over on her tongue, wonders, then, what to do, to leave it in the bowl & flush it down or perhaps a burial, but this is impossible, there is no patch of ground she calls her own, nothing except the twin tomato plants on the balcony & the pot of leggy geraniums (survivors of winter). Should she feed it to the geraniums or, perhaps, eat it herself, strange sushi? Or should she push down the metal handle, watch the swirl and rush as it's flushed out of the apartment, the house, shunted through metal tubes away from her to somewhere she can never reach, somewhere under the street, where it will lodge, gathering and collecting with shit, blood, cigarette butts, other lost children? The lights are out now.

viii. Anniversary

All matter
decayed
the leaves once red
now burnt beside
the wrought-iron gate

nothing mattered
the alphabets were changed

No one could love her better
you said *no one would do it*
differently

*

Is there nothing to do
but take the compost out
to the driveway
the neighbour's son
has blocked with his pickup?

Someone dropped a condom
like a burst balloon from a birthday
party that will never take place

all the guests are unborn

Why are you holding your heart open
over the compost heap
over the condom in the driveway?

Why do you insist on picking it up?

*

The woman who drowned her two
on Tuesday because it was
Tuesday

or in Arkansas the bird-girl born
the size of her father's fist

Her mother said *he can put*
her in his pocket
beside his watch beside
his ticking heart

*

A figure on the altar is thinned
by the touch of the supplicants

so a daughter's body disappears under
her mother's hand

*

Is there nothing to do
but wait   love
beside the driveway
beside the river to
another bleached sea?

Shred the fresh-inked news
fill the pots of tomato plants
because there is no other soil?

Show me one story —
one story —
in which what is promised
bears fruit —

*

The beach almost entirely of clamshells
broken, a heron parting water

we refuse to give up

Nothing   love
could make me leave
you   nothing
though my body has broken
beneath yours a thousand times
& after each we come up
for air forgetting
what we sought

oh the parting
oh the sea battering its slow
swollen heart

another name for any sorrow we share
is happiness —

ix. After Her

You ask for a light
& it is given
though the hand that offers
is singed with flame.

Why do you turn
to walk alone
in a garden
thick with bees
& still count
the steps as if they led
away from grief?

Somewhere, your sister
can find only
the one child
who will never be enough.

Somewhere, your husband
moves in smoke between bees
learning whatever dance
the smoke will teach.

x. The Wife's Account

Here's what happened: At lunch your mother gave me one

of those tapes She has a whole library — have you seen them

in her closet? lose weight impotent no more grief divorce —

I'm driving home on Marine Drive & I pop the tape in

The first thing it says *Do not operate a motor*

vehicle while listening to this recording I pulled into

the parking lot at Jericho — across the inlet, mountains

on the mountains, snow, in June, intractable — I rolled

the window down, tilted back the seat & the curing tape began

playing the sound of waves striking beach I kept listening —

seems ridiculous now — still just the sound of recorded

waves echoing & repeating the waves on the beach outside the car

That's when I got out, left the tape playing, I guess I left the car unlocked & walked toward the sea's uttering

then turned to cross the parking lot, the road, climbing

two by two the stairs to the edge of woods — you know that trail

where we sometimes walk — From the top I saw the car

still idling far away & small as a shell you'd lift to your ear

The woods deep green at that time of day, but the dark

runnelled bark, the red mud trail lit by setting light & everywhere

anemone green lace — I never noticed before — as if

sea once flooded woods then withdrew, leaving seaweed looped

over branches & logs, across rocks & decaying forest floor

I didn't stop walking & a distant, persistent ringing —

which might have been the alarm since when I

came out of those woods, much later, in the dark, the car was gone

xi.

Straw hat. Sandy tiles.
This month's blood
on the beach
towels where
we made love having
swum too far, too fast.

Our daughter's hair was cornsilk.

I want you back.

Flies in the kitchen.
Dog asleep since before
you left.

Nothing's as easy
as despair.

Most of the sugar's stuck
to the bottom of the glass.

xii.

Squinting below the blinds:

down here, it's . . . well, down here.

Maybe the eyes are tired or

maybe the womb is tired or maybe

the dog — old in his bones — asleep

on 4 cool squares of tile.

Because light comes straight off

the water — & can't help it. Because

the prescribed lenses are weighted, meaning

the user has to blink. Because yesterday

you brought an armful of honeysuckle —

summer's sweet propaganda —

untangling the branches:

a stem in the water doesn't meet the same stem

above water: it's an optical thing. I've spent

most of my life underwater, trying to

make ends meet. Then you come along, air creature,

making it look easy to breathe.

xiii. Mrs. Barlowe's Plum Tree

All summer the grass grows long
in the school yard across from Mrs. Barlowe's lawn

where the plums in the plum tree ripen

All summer I walk past to gauge
their purpling
until one August evening
their flesh is bruised as twilight
Plums heavy with their own
possibility

When Mrs. Barlowe sees me she
descends the steps from the porch

one hand on the rail
one hand on her cane

*My son is coming to pick them
as soon as they ripen*

Mrs. Barlowe nods to the school yard
past the chain-link fence &

two empty soccer goals expectant
as two women

*I'd offer them to you but my son
would be disappointed*

She goes back up the steps closes
the door
I pick the plums for her

dropping them one by one
into the bucket

Tomorrow she'll tell me her son came

xiv.

Actually there were crows on the branches
of the plum tree
purple-feathered in the twilight

The Sufis say the bird that flew
to look for paradise finally found it
in a mirror

These are not plums you'd put
in the fridge leaving a note to your lover
These plums taste like lemons
Evil plums   Stepmother plums

Last time D went shopping
there were eight different kinds of pepper
on his list

Who needs eight different kinds of pepper?

The point is he does the shopping

There is no Mrs. Barlowe

The Egyptian hieroglyph for mother

is the same as the one for death
a lappet-faced vulture

That tree belongs to no one
but the crows

& even they won't eat the plums

There is no plum tree
After I dreamt it
I cut it down

xv. Building Her Tomb

If the stone blocks
cut from our quarries
had been any larger,
our carts would not have
hauled them.

Any smaller
it would have taken
too many years
too many lives
the queen dead
before her death had been prepared.

As it was the tombs could be built
in time.

Experience taught us
the dimensions of our lives.

Pushed from my mother
they began to cut
stone for my tomb.

My life lived
in a lengthening shadow
while a servant served tea
the way I liked,
a little bit of honey on the spoon.

xvi. The Pharaoh on His Deathbed

This bed too big for me
Pillow against my back
like a wife
She always wanted what I
couldn't give
Not enough to visit friends
we had to talk about it afterwards
Not enough to eat a bird
We had to know how we felt
For me the bird in my mouth
a bird for her something else
She had nostalgia for a moment
as it was happening
hoping I suppose
that it would mean something
Each morning I rose
slipping the thermometer under
her tongue
We watched mercury rise
by degrees
She wanted a reason
I wanted a son

xvii.

the light walk up the road.
no one goes there.
no one except him.
who has clouded.
who has clouded & stayed
& left too.
who is just so
& so. who has taken the walk
up the hill
alone & out of his mind
& difficult.
who has found the path the children
took to the playground.
the children now grown up or
gone & none to replace them.
who hears the metal bars rattle when
the wind blows &
rain beats a hollow hollow.
who has scattered blessings & curses
& a certain whimpering.
who steps one foot in front
of another foot up the path between
the alder trees in a web of sunlight.
who flinches in the sunlight. foot

& then foot & then foot again.
who flinches
who when what moves through him
replaces what has been there &
only no one stays.
except him who has been cruel
& loved. & loved again.

xviii. Intention

Though it outlasted the bombs
that fell on that church in 1943
the coat of egg to make its colours
shine (sometime in the 18th century)
though only every other granule
of paint from his brush remains &
what we see there is a '   '
of his intention

Because of or in spite of
this, she restores the wall

Still Christ's hands over
the table, still the rapt
faces & now her face
this woman whose lips nearly
kiss the stone so close is her breath
to that inch where wax or soot or web interposed
May its vanishing be illuminated
May the last meal fill with light
Lover of the world, taste the world in its going

xix.

You will be earth
then you can rest
stop this ceaseless
river of words &
the small fires lit
beside their banks.
Wake, little ones in your
thick blue swaddling
this morning brings another lesson:
how to kindle flame
from the bones
of the heart.
Wake,
after the waking
after the lessons
& the river
& the fires lit
then you will be earth
then you can rest
stop this ceaseless river
of words & the small fires —

xx.

Body does not love mind
because it will not
shut up, will not shut up
will not stop: *If you don't give him*
a baby
he's going to leave us both.

xxi.

What did you wish for?

      I didn't wish, I waited.

Waited?

      For my life to begin.

& did it begin?

      Afterwards I thought it must
      have.

Why?

      Didn't I wake to footfalls
      on the roof, like
      rain? Didn't I know

      it was the pregnant skunk
      who sleeps under the tea rose?

xxii.   *As Surely as the Dead*

As surely as the dead
tulips their
stems triumphant
having poked up through
wilted petals

they did not finish
their last meal
water still luminous
in the vase half-empty
on the bedside table

beside your glasses
that catch street-
light through slatted blinds
reflecting phases of the moon
onto our walls

above the bed where you
are dreaming
(later you will tell me)
that dream from childhood
the world made known
not by word or name

but by its heaviness
each object — bed table
lamp carpet — split
into molecules whose weight & vibration
stand in
for any meaning

as the heart will beat
(you promised me)
long after we've declared it
broken

when you woke you said all this
searching for the path back
into dream-clarity

when you woke you
began with the blown-open blossoms
of dead tulips
you said

Radiance

xxiii. The Naming

Begin with the table & the sea beyond
                                        begin with morning
Begin with the hand moving across the page
                                        the sky's Cyrillic
Begin with the bees who quit the honey-suckled
dew-beloved earth, bees gone sour into themselves
                                        I begin before you wake
begin writing for the first time, after a long time,
                                        begin at the whitewood
. table staring past the rocks to the sea

Begin with a chair   Begin with a table

Begin to say something   (to say not nothing)
                                to whisper in your ear the names
of things, unspeakable —
                                white clouds mass over the mountains
as a clam clings to the dark rock, here on the writing table

Finger bones begin to do the diligent work of pen against page
not so hard the ink runs   not so light it can't be read

Begin writing of the man who put his ear to the comb-packed
box & said he knew the song the bees sang, song

for the dead queen

Begin before Christ, in China, the year 500
during The Rectification of Names
                              The robed monks
carrying thick scrolls lift their robes & bend
to each flower in the field, calling it by its known name
                              They list that name in a table

                                        Begin to name &
where there is confusion ascribe one name, the right name

Name trees, rivers, forms of love & weather
                              also jealousies & hates, rages, motives, ideas
Name the dark animals of the mind
                              How else to maintain order?

As I begin to write to you, my love, a finch lights on a pine branch
that bows to its burden, scholar to his master

                    Begin with the tide coming in, the heart reaching out
to the end of itself
                              & calling & calling
                                        tide filling the inlet, the wound
that cannot be healed
                              (you doubt the wound?)

I begin with the table & the sea, beyond
                              devil's paintbrush at the golden hour

                    Sing the song for our own green dead

Nothing forgets us
                    not the animal who looked at me & blinked
before she slipped from the rocks back into the water

xxiv. In Which We Resume

this time the ratchet &
the socket wrench
this time without looking back
this time, you loose under
me, grass still on your skin, scent of sunscreen
& insect repellent
this time without training wheels
with our eyes open, *look, ma, no hands* —
this time without spite & despite warnings &
your spit in my mouth
this time backwards & keep your hat on
this time busy fingers, all thumbs, do that again
this time the national anthem or a harmonica
this time roll the windows down so I can stick my feet out

xxv.

Whatever the light that first
morning I found you
in my kitchen drinking coffee
with sour milk
a square of sun on the floor
blue from ice that glazed the window
Whatever the grief —
child of losses I cut that morning
like branches of the quince tree
still burdened with snow
Whatever woke you
Whatever blue light is given
to remember your back bent
over the sink
Whatever the chance
another morning like that gift
of whatever happenstance
brought us the nightingale drunk
on first light
or the tracks switching
at the railway crossing
on gears timed to make sun rise
whatever song the wheels sang
to accompany those green branches
hissing in fire —

xxvi.   Train Window

Dawn on the train, my face
pressed against rocking

glass. Your head leaning on
my shoulder, hands in my lap, you

reach for sleep made difficult
by grief or love. Outside

bare birch. A glacial
river enunciates the cold.

Sometimes the nest of an eagle, but
never the eagle.

Raw sliver of sunlight breaks
between mountains. It pierces the window,

articulating a space between
our bodies.

After we lost the child, I picked up
the uncarved pumpkin &

cut it in half, raking fingers through the saffron
flesh, loosening the seeds.

I was going to salt & roast them, but
forgot, leaving them in a bowl on the counter

where they sprouted. A handful
of long shoots, expectant

lifting their shells on small green shoulders, craving
light. Each meal we prepared we

watched them, delirious with their own
growing, eating themselves

to stay alive. One morning they were
limp & straggly, draped over the lip

of the bowl, like mountain climbers who expire
in thin air, leaving their slumped bodies on the top

of the world.
The other day, stepping

out of the shower, mist around your
hips & shoulders, you let yourself

smile *What are we going to do*
with this love?

The train stops. A freight's in trouble
further up the track & we are frozen

on steel spanning another river.
Ahead where the air is thinner

we cannot see. Behind
we can't turn back.

What are we going to do
with this love? Sun roses snow

on the branches. I lift my face from
the window glass.

We're tied to each other.
Where you climb, I will

climb. This light, ungraspable,
all we have.

Acknowledgements

The epigraph is taken from Theodore Roethke's "The Lost Son."

"Notorious" is based on images from Hitchcock's film of the same name and from newspaper accounts of the Scandinavian skier who came back to life after freezing to death in an icy river.

"Over Coffee" is for Miranda Pearson with thanks for her company in poetry.
"Occupant" is for P. K. Page.
"The Naming" is for Gina Ogilvie and Ian Scott.

The author gratefully acknowledges the assistance of the Canada Council & the B.C. Arts Council.

Some of these poems were published in a slightly different form in: *Salmagundi*, *Queen Street Quarterly*, *CV2*, & in the anthology *Mocambo Nights: Poetry from the Mocambo Readings* (Ekstasis, ed. Patrick Lane).

Much thanks to my editor, Michael Redhill.
To Michael Ondaatje.
To Martha Sharpe & Adrienne Leahey at Anansi.
To Angel, in advance. To Linda Spalding.

This book is for Douglas.

Jericho, August 2001.